YOUR KNOWLEDGE HAS VALUE

- We will publish your bachelor's and
  master's thesis, essays and papers

- Your own eBook and book -
  sold worldwide in all relevant shops

- Earn money with each sale

Upload your text at www.GRIN.com
and publish for free

Data Encryption Standard (DES) and Issues of DES and its Replacement

Haitham Ismail

Bibliographic information published by the German National Library:

The German National Library lists this publication in the National Bibliography; detailed bibliographic data are available on the Internet at http://dnb.dnb.de.

ISBN: 9783346728760
This book is also available as an ebook.

© GRIN Publishing GmbH
Nymphenburger Straße 86
80636 München

Print and binding: Books on Demand GmbH, Norderstedt, Germany
Printed on acid-free paper from responsible sources.

The present work has been carefully prepared. Nevertheless, authors and publishers do not incur liability for the correctness of information, notes, links and advice as well as any printing errors.

GRIN web shop: https://www.grin.com/document/1264836

A Complete overview over Data Encryption Standard (DES)

Haitham Ismail

Table of Contents

Table of Figures

Introduction

The business Management system (BMS) is a powerful management tool that helps an organization's management build, create, control, and monitor business activities. Currently, it evolved and has become the backbone of strategic planning and everyday business operations. BMS has the technical infrastructure, such as access control, to protect information from unauthorized access. Still, it cannot be used alone to preserve the confidentiality and integrity of information handled against different challenges such as secure system development and maintenance, operation and physical security and compliance with regulations (Stankov & Tsochev, 2020). Cryptography plays an essential role in protecting data's confidentiality and integrity, which might be hosted within the companies' premises or outsourced to a cloud service. Furthermore, cryptography protect information processed and transmitted within a communication medium.

BMS incorporates many algorithms that serve this purpose; however, some of them are legacy or obsolete, such as RC2, RC4, DES, 3DES, MD2, MD4, MD5, SHA-1, and no longer recommended to be used because they are proved to be vulnerable. This report will select one of these obsolete cryptographic algorithms, analyze it, discuss one of its vulnerabilities, and suggest a modern algorithm to address this weakness.

Cryptographic algorithm selection

As a result of the contribution between IBM and the National Bureau of Standard (NBS), an encryption algorithm called Data Encryption Standard (DES) saw the light in 1977. In 2022, DES is considered an outdated algorithm because of the advances in computational power and sophisticated attacker techniques. Thus, many weaknesses have been discovered. Nevertheless, it is crucial to study DES because it is considered the basis of other advanced algorithms

(Highland, 1987). Thus, DES algorithms will be selected to discuss, analyse, and find their

modern replacement in this report.

Data Encryption Standard

Symmetric encryption Algorithm

Let us imagine that two parties are exchanging information over a communication medium. If

the exchange message is in plaintext (See **Fehler! Verweisquelle konnte nicht gefunden**

werden.), the information is not protected against eavesdropping and man-in-the-middle attacks,

and it needs encryption to be protected. The encrypted data transmitted through a

communication media is called ciphertext, generated using a secret key within an encryption

algorithm. However, another secret key is used to decrypt the ciphertext at the receiver side and

extract the original plaintext message unaltered (Buchanan, 2017; Denning, 1982).

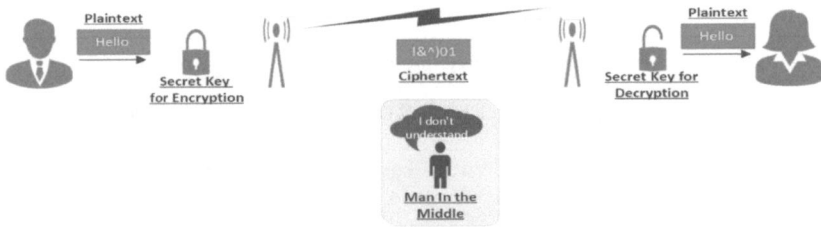

Figure 1 - Encryption and decryption process Note: "Author's own work"

The secret key must be shared between the sender and the receiver before they can exchange any

information. When the secret key is the same for encryption and decryption, it is called

symmetric key encryption. The cryptographic algorithm used with the symmetric key must be

two-way so that the receiver can retrieve the plain text from the message received (Buchanan,

2017). Thus, the primary role of encryption in cyber security systems is to protect data stored or

transmitted.

3

DES Encryption Key

DES is a block cipher symmetric key encryption algorithm that divides data into 64- bit blocks.

It uses a 56-bit symmetric key for encryption and decryption, which gives 2^56 or

72,057,594,037,927,936 or 72 million billion possible keys.

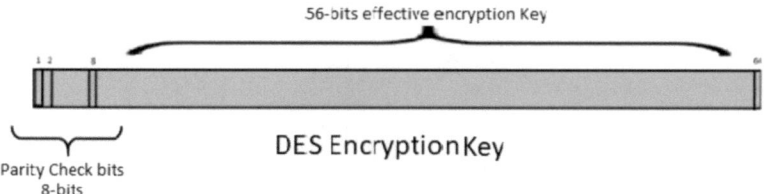

Figure 2 - DES 56-bit Encryption key. Note: "Author's own work"

Furthermore, an 8-bits parity check is included within the key to verify its integrity (Huang, 2008

as cited in Afolabi & Atanda, 2016), which means one parity check every 8 bits. For instance,

the parity checks bits namely are numbered by 8,16,24,32,40,48,56,64 in the encryption 64-bit.

Therefore, the effective encryption key is 56-bits (See Figure 2).

DES Encryption Subkeys

The data block is encrypted in 16 successive rounds of encryption using 16 encryption 48-bit

subkeys derived from the original 56-bit encryption key through a series of permutations,

substitution and shifting (See Figure 3) to produce 64-bit ciphertext (J. Orlin Grabbe, 2006;

Singh et al., 2010).

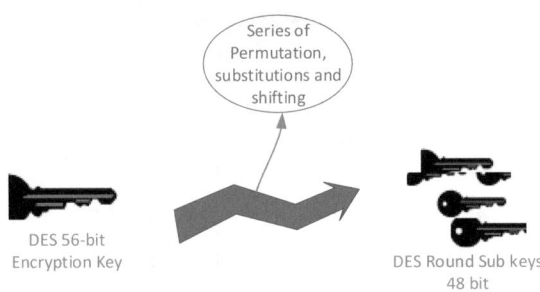

Figure 3 - 16 Round Subkeys are derived from the original DES 56-bit key. Note: "Author's own work"

The round subkeys are generated based on Feistel networks with either contracting or expanding

round functions (Hoang, V. and Rogaway, P. as cited in Rabin, 2010) to obscure the relationship

between the subkeys that encrypt data blocks and the primary DES encryption key.

How does DES Work?

In DES, data is broken into small blocks of 64-bit or 16 hexadecimal numbers and produces 64-

bit ciphertext blocks (See Figure 4). However, it is common to have the last block contain less

than 64-bit of data as not all sizes can be divisible by 64. Consequently, it adds padding bits to

complete the 64-bit size of the last data block. Then, it processes each block separately

depending on the encryption mode of operation. The plaintext blocks are initially permuted with

(P-boxes) to shuffle the input bits, making the relation between plaintext and ciphertext difficult

to colorate and understand (Grabbe, 2006). Then, the resulted bits are encrypted through 16

5

rounds of encryption using 16 encryption subkeys generated from the original DES encryption key. Finally, the resulted bits are permuted inversely to have a final ciphertext.

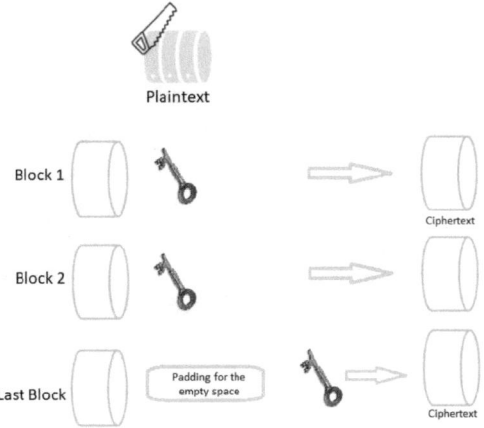

Figure 4 – Block Encryption - Note: "Author's own work"

DES Vulnerabilities

In general, cryptanalysis studies cracking ciphers to get plaintext or key from the ciphertext. A case in point, DES depends on a 56-bit key of possible 72 million billion possible keys, which is considered limited, especially with advancements in the computing field. Thus, relatively limited key space made the algorithm vulnerable to a brute-force attack (See Figure 5). Likewise, a cipher can also be breakable if we get the encryption key from the plaintext – ciphertext pairs (Denning, 1982). We need to try all possible keys to encrypt a known text encrypted before with DES and then compare ciphertexts. If it matches, we succeed in cracking the key. This process is called an exhaustive search for a key.

Figure 5 - It is time to try all the possible keys to crack DES and get the DES encryption key.

Note: Adapted from Baker (2018)

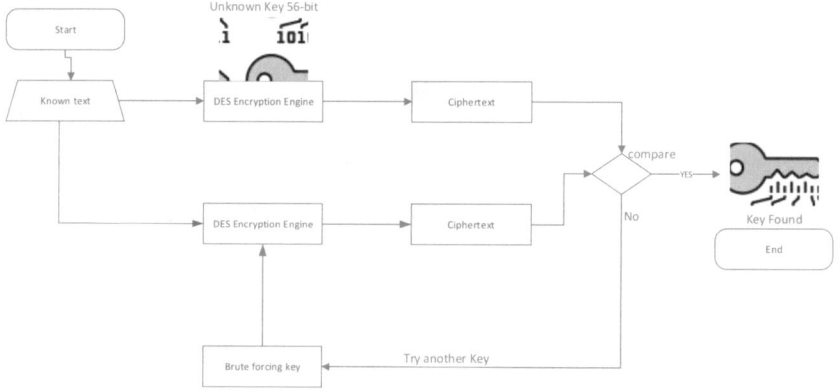

Figure 6 – DES Brute-force flow chart diagram - Note: "Author's own work"

Brute-force

This attack requires a lot of processing power that was not feasible in the 70s, 80s and 90s.

However, it is available today in feasible time and money with the advancement of central

processing units (CPUs) in 2022 (See Figure 7Figure 7 - Published DES Brute-force attempt

time taken). The most famous attempt to crack DES was proven to be true when it was

announced that a 56-bit was successfully cracked in 56 hours using a dedicated computing

device called the Deep Crack in only 56 hours on July 17, 1998, by John Glamore and Paul

Kocher (Markoff, 1998). They built a homemade computer with 27 boards containing 64 chips

that test almost 90 billion keys per second. However, other attempts were recorded in history, as

shown in Figure 7.

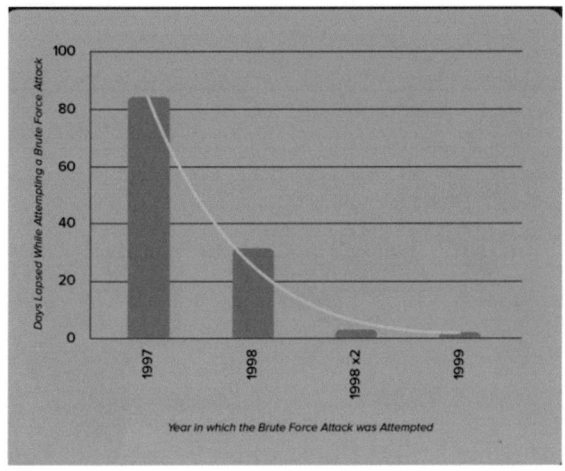

Figure 7 - Published DES Brute-force attempt time taken (Larson, 2014)

Parallel Processing.

The cryptanalysis of modern ciphers needs high computational power (Possible 2^{56}

computational operation in the case of DES key search). The task to find the right DES key can

8

be distributed among processing units (e.g. computer cluster or dedicated computing device).

Kumar et al. (2006) mentioned that the possible keyspace could be distributed among nodes or processing units that work in parallel to find the right key in the least time possible. They used Field Programmable Gate Arrays (FPGAs) as it is relatively cheaper than a regular CPU or computer. The device is designed to include four search units in each FPGA that can check four keys every 10ns, while it includes 120 FPGA.

Each key search unit tries a key to compare the DES ciphertext of a known plaintext, which was encrypted by the unknown DES key, with the cipher resulting from the plaintext encryption by the secret key used from the dedicated part of the keyspace in the search unit (Kumar et al., 2006). Consequently, the device can check $4*120 = 480$ keys for every 10ns. Therefore, the approximate time for finding the correct key is 2^{56} possible keys divided by 480 ns, 8.7 days.

Advanced Encryption Algorithm

Many encryption algorithms were developed to overcome DES's weakness. Advanced Encryption Standard (AES) was announced to be trusted by the National Institute of Technology (NIST) in 2001 (Buchanan, 2017). It is a symmetric block cipher as it uses the same key for encryption and decryption. In addition, it made it exponentially far harder to brute-force the key as it happened with DES because it uses a larger keyspace of a 128-bit or 192-bit, or 256-bit key (Bhat et al., 2015). However, performance-wise, AES consumes more battery and time than DES because of its larger key and higher number of round encryption series on the data block (See Figure 8). The difference in performance is found when encrypting a larger block size (Al-Tamimi, 2022). Therefore, all these enhancements have nominated AES to be used instead of DES in all applications.

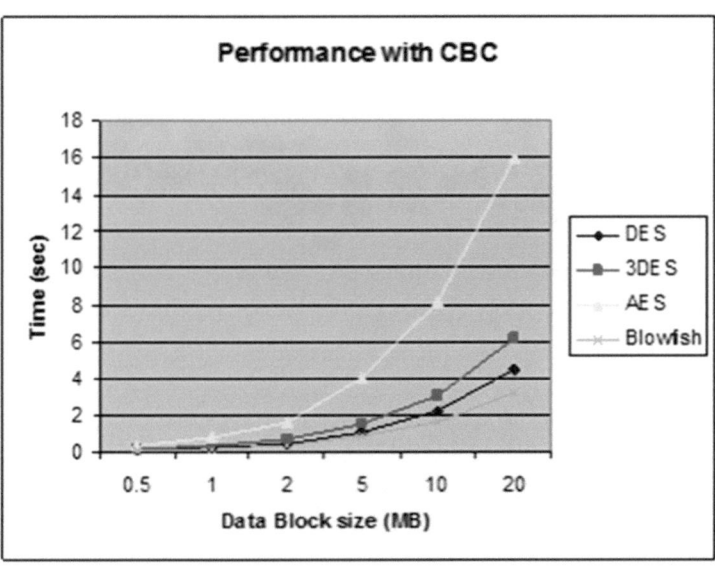

Figure 8 - Performance chart comparison for DES, AES and another Encryption Algorithm in CBC mode of operations(Al-Tamimi, 2022).

The size of the data block for different versions of AES is 128-bit, while the number of rounds of encryption for the block is either 10 (128-bit Key) or 12 (192-bit Key) or 16 (256-bit Key) (Abdullah, 2017). The variable key gives the algorithm the capability to have different versions used for different applications based on the hardware.

Conclusion and Comparison Summary.

DES is vulnerable to brute-force attacks because of its relatively limited key size, which nowadays is feasible considering the available computational power in the market. Thus, AES came as a replacement, mainly because its larger key size allows it to fit in different applications. A summary of the main differences can be shown in the following table.

	Data Encryption Standard (DES)	Advanced Encryption Standard (AES)
Developed date	1977	2001
Key Length	56 bits	128-bit or 192-bit or 256-bit
Type of cipher	Symertric block cipher	Symertric block cipher
Block size	64 bits	128 bits
Security	It proved to be cracked through brute force activities	No known successful attack
Power and time consumption	Lower	Higher

References

Abdullah, A. M. (2017). Advanced encryption standard (AES) algorithm to encrypt and decrypt data. *Cryptography and Network Security, 16*, 1-11.

Afolabi, A., & Atanda, a. (2016). Comparative Analysis of some Selected Cryptographic Algorithms. *Computing Information Systems, Development Informatics& Allied Research Journal, volume 7*, 41-57.

Al-Tamimi, A.-K. (2022). Performance Analysis of Data Encryption Algorithms.

Baker, J. (2018). *Brute Force.* https://i.redd.it/ce4j9153osc71.jpg

Bhat, B., Ali, A. W., & Gupta, A. (2015, 15-16 May 2015). DES and AES performance evaluation. International Conference on Computing, Communication & Automation,

Buchanan, W. J. (2017). *Cryptography.* River Publishers. http://ebookcentral.proquest.com/lib/ecu/detail.action?docID=5050193

Denning, D. E. R. (1982). *Cryptography and data security.* Addison-Wesley Longman Publishing Co., Inc.

Grabbe. (2006). The DES Algorithm Illustrated. *Laissez Faire City Times, 2*(28).

Grabbe, J. O. (2006). The DES Algorithm Illustrated.

Highland, H. (1987). Data encryption standard II? *Computers & Security, 6*(3), 195-196. https://doi.org/https://doi.org/10.1016/0167-4048(87)90095-2

Kumar, S. S., Paar, C., Pelzl, J., Pfeiffer, G., & Schimmler, M. (2006). Breaking Ciphers with COPACOBANA - A Cost-Optimized Parallel Code Breaker. CHES,

Larson, M. (2014). *WHAT ARE THE DIFFERENCES BETWEEN DES AND AES ENCRYPTION?* Townsend Security. https://info.townsendsecurity.com/bid/72450/what-are-the-differences-between-des-and-aes-encryption

Markoff, J. (1998). U.S. Data-Scrambling Code Cracked With Homemade Equipment. *The New York Times.* https://archive.nytimes.com/www.nytimes.com/library/tech/98/07/biztech/articles/17encrypt.html

Rabin, T. (2010). *Advances in Cryptology – CRYPTO 2010.* Springer, Berlin, Heidelberg. https://doi.org/https://doi-org.ezproxy.ecu.edu.au/10.1007/978-3-642-14623-7

Singh, D. R., Ramveer, & Ojha, D. E. O. (2010). AN ORDEAL RANDOM DATA ENCRYPTION SCHEME (ORDES). *International Journal of Engineering Science and Technology, 2.*

Stankov, I., & Tsochev, G. (2020). Vulnerability and Protection of Business Management Systems: Threats and Challenges. *PROBLEMS OF ENGINEERING CYBERNETICS AND ROBOTICS, 72.* https://doi.org/10.7546/PECR.72.20.04